THE POWER OF POSITIVE AGING

EMBRACING LIFE AFTER FIFTY

DR. MINAKSHI BANSAL

DEDICATION

This book is dedicated to all who believe in the beauty and potential of aging. To those who see their later years not as a time of winding down, but as a grand, new adventure filled with opportunities for growth, discovery, and deeper connections.

To my parents, whose grace in aging continues to inspire and guide me, teaching me the true meaning of strength and resilience.

And to future generations, may you embrace every stage of your life with courage and joy, and may you find in your journey all the wisdom and fulfillment that I have found in writing this book.

❦❦❦

Contents

Prayer   *vii*

About The Author   *ix*

Preface   *xiii*

1. Redefining Aging   1

Part 1

2. The Joy Of Lifelong Learning   7

Part 2

3. Physical Health After Fifty   13

Part 3

4. Strategies For Fostering Mental Health, Including Mindfulness, Meditation,   19

Part 4

5. Social Butterflies: Staying Connected   25

Part 5

6. Harnessing Experience   31

Part 6

7. Financial Fitness For Later Life   37

Part 7

8. Embracing Technology   43

Part 8

9. The Adventure Begins At Retirement   49

Part 9

10. Volunteering: Giving Back   55

Part 10

11. The Art Of Hobbies   61

Part 11

Contents

12. Mindset Matters   67

Part 12

13. Home Sweet Home   73

Part 13

14. Navigating Health Care   79

Part 14

15. The Legacy We Leave   85

Part 15

16. Fashion And Self-Expression After Fifty   91

Part 16

17. Nutrition For Longevity   97

Part 17

18. Staying Safe   103

Part 18

19. Intergenerational Bonds   109

Part 19

20. Celebrating Milestones   115

Part 20

21. SUMMARY   121

Citation and References   125

Other Books of The Author   127

Contact   129

Prayer

"Om Bhadram Karnebhih Shrinuyama Devah
Bhadram Pashyemakshabhiryajatrah
Sthirairangais Tushtuvamsastanubhih
Vyashema Devahitam Yadayuh
Svasti Na Indro Vriddhashravah
Svasti Nah Pusha Vishwavedah
Svasti Nastarkshyo Arishtanemih
Svasti No Brihaspatir Dadhatu
Om Shantih Shantih Shantih"

This mantra is a prayer for universal well-being, invoking the blessings of various deities for protection, health, and happiness. It emphasizes the importance of experiencing the auspicious through all senses and living a life aligned with divine purpose. The repetition of "Shantih" at the end signifies a deep desire for peace in the individual, the environment, and the universe at large. This mantra is often recited as a prayer for peace, prosperity, and the physical and spiritual well-being of all beings.

About The Author

Dr. Minakshi Bansal, born in the bustling metropolis of Delhi, India, has led a life steeped in artistry, scholarly pursuit, and an unwavering commitment to societal betterment. Following her marriage, she relocated to Ahmedabad, Gujarat, where she has since blossomed into a multifaceted beacon of inspiration for many. Dr. Minakshi is not only recognized as a gifted artist in the realm of Fine Arts but also as an esteemed author, a devoted social worker and a dedicated research scholar in Psychology. Her journey, marked by a profound dedication to elevating those around her, especially the downtrodden and underprivileged children of society, is a testament to her deep-seated belief in the transformative power of engagement and empathy.

From her earliest days, Minakshi was distinguished by an insatiable appetite for reading. Her literary universe was inhabited by characters and narratives that spanned ethical tales, motivational and inspirational stories, and the mythic parables imbued with life lessons. This voracious reading habit was not merely for personal edification but was driven by a desire to distill and disseminate the essence of these narratives to foster the development of students and peers alike. She was particularly captivated by the lives and teachings of historical figures and spiritual leaders such as Adi Shankaracharya, Swami Vivekananda, Dr. APJ Abdul Kalam, Mahamana Pandit Madan Mohan Malviya, Mahatma Gandhi, Sardar Vallabhai Patel, and Vinoba Bhave, among others. Their philosophies and life stories fueled her ambition to embody their ideals of resilience, selflessness, and relentless pursuit of knowledge.

Dr. Minakshi's academic and practical engagement with psychology has been equally noteworthy. As a research scholar, her focus has been on exploring the intricate tapestry of the human psyche, aiming to unlock the potential for psychological well-being and societal harmony. Her scholarly work is complemented by her active involvement in social work, where she employs her academic insights to make tangible differences in the lives of the underprivileged. Her endeavours in social work are characterized by an innovative approach that combines traditional wisdom with contemporary psychological practices to address the multifaceted challenges faced by these communities.

Her artistic talents, another facet of her diverse capabilities, are not merely a personal passion but also serve as a medium through which she communicates and connects with others. Her art, rich in symbolism and emotional depth, reflects her philosophical inquiries and social concerns, offering viewers a glimpse into the breadth of her intellect and the depth of her compassion.

In addition to her contributions to the arts and social sciences, Dr. Minakshi has embraced the healing arts of Pranic Healing, mastering the techniques developed by Master Choa Kok Sui. This practice, which focuses on the manipulation of Prana or life energy to heal the body and aura, has been both a personal journey of discovery and a means through which she extends her healing touch to others. Her proficiency in Pranic Healing is complemented by her advocacy and teaching of various forms of meditation aimed at rejuvenation, personal betterment, and the cultivation of harmony within individuals and communities alike.

Dr. Minakshi's life is a narrative of relentless pursuit, not just of personal achievement but of the upliftment and empowerment of society at large. Her diverse interests and talents—spanning the arts, literature, psychology, and the healing practices—converge on a singular path of service. She embodies the spirit of the luminaries who inspired her, channelling their legacy through her actions and teachings. Through her books, art, and social initiatives, she continues to inspire a new generation to embark on their own journeys of self-discovery, resilience, and altruism.

Her commitment to social betterment, particularly her focus on uplifting underprivileged children, reflects a deep understanding of the transformative potential of education and personal development. By integrating her knowledge of psychology, her artistic sensibilities, and her healing practices, Dr. Bansal has developed a holistic approach to social work that addresses both the immediate needs and the long-term well-being of the communities she serves.

As an author, Dr. Minakshi's writings offer a blend of inspirational insights, practical wisdom, and reflective contemplations drawn from her extensive reading and life experiences. Her books serve as a guide for those seeking to navigate the complexities of life with grace, resilience, and purpose. Through her narratives, she extends an invitation to her readers to explore the depths of their own potential and to contribute meaningfully to the collective well-being of society.

In Dr. Minakshi Bansal, we find a remarkable synthesis of the artist, the scholar, the healer, and the social activist. Her life's work stands as a beacon of hope and a source of inspiration for individuals seeking to make a difference in the world. Her story is a compelling reminder of the power of individual action, rooted in compassion and driven by a profound commitment to the betterment of humanity. Dr. Minakshi's legacy is not just in the tangible outcomes of her efforts but in the enduring spirit of inquiry, empathy, and service that she embodies.

$$\wp\wp\wp$$

Preface

As I sit to write this preface, I am struck by the profound journey that life presents, especially as we cross into the latter half of our years. It is a time often marked by reflection and anticipation—reflection on the decades past and anticipation of what is yet to come. This book, "The Power of Positive Aging: Embracing Life After Fifty," is born from both personal and observed experiences, a testament to the remarkable potential that the senior years hold for each of us.

The genesis of this book came from countless conversations with peers, witnessing the struggles and triumphs of family members, and my professional interactions with those who are navigating the complexities of aging. Each story shared with me was a thread in the rich tapestry of wisdom and challenges that seniors face today. What struck me most was the resilience and the unyielding desire to live fully, no matter the number of years.

As we age, we often confront a societal narrative that focuses heavily on decline and loss. This narrative can overshadow the many opportunities for growth, joy, and continued achievement that are also present in later life. I wrote this book to challenge that narrative, to shine a light on the positive aspects of aging, and to provide a guide for making the most of these enriching years.

Throughout this book, I have woven together research, expert opinions, and real-life stories to offer a comprehensive look at how we can age with vitality and purpose. The chapters are designed to address the physical, mental, emotional, and social aspects of aging, with practical advice on navigating each area effectively.

The concept of positive aging is central to this text. It is a perspective that encourages us to approach aging as a natural and enriching phase of life, one that is full of potential rather than decline. This mindset is not about denying the challenges that aging can bring but about facing these challenges with a proactive and optimistic outlook.

We delve into topics such as the importance of maintaining physical health through tailored exercise and nutrition, the benefits of engaging the mind continually through learning and hobbies, and the critical role of social connections in sustaining our spirits. The book also explores the changing relationship we have with work and finances, the transformative power of technology in our lives, and the deep satisfaction that can come from giving back to the community.

Moreover, "The Power of Positive Aging" tackles the subject of legacy—an integral part of our later years. It prompts readers to contemplate the memories and impacts they wish to leave behind, emphasizing that legacy is not only about material assets but also the values, wisdom, and spirit we pass on to others.

Writing this book has been a journey of discovery and affirmation. It reaffirmed my belief that aging is not merely about survival but about thriving. It has reinforced my conviction that the later years can be some of the most rewarding and active years of one's life if approached with the right knowledge and attitude.

To all readers, whether you are approaching fifty, are well into your seventies, or somewhere in between, this book is for you. It is also for those who support and love older adults—a guide to help you understand the dynamics at play as your loved ones enter this phase of their lives.

It is my hope that "The Power of Positive Aging" serves as both a beacon and a guide, illuminating the path to a fulfilling and vibrant later life. May you find within its pages the inspiration and practical advice to not only face the challenges of aging but to embrace the myriad opportunities it presents.

Let us redefine what it means to grow older. Let us embrace the power of positive aging together, transforming our later years into a period of unprecedented growth and joy. Thank you for joining me on this remarkable journey.

Dr. Minakshi Bansal
Social Activist
Ahmedabad, Gujarat, Bharat

❦❦❦

ONE

REDEFINING AGING

Aging is a universal experience—a journey that every human being embarks on from the moment they are born. Despite its inevitability, the way people perceive aging varies greatly across different cultures. These perceptions shape how individuals feel about getting older and significantly influence the quality of life experienced by older adults. By understanding and transforming these views, societies can improve not only the lives of the elderly but also the health of their communities.

In many Western societies, aging is often viewed through a negative lens. It's frequently associated with loss—loss of youth, physical strength, and mental sharpness. This perspective can lead to ageism, a form of discrimination that impacts job opportunities, social activities, and even healthcare for older adults. The media often reinforces these stereotypes by portraying older individuals as out of touch, frail, or burdensome. However, these views are not universal and can be changed to foster a more positive and respectful understanding of aging.

Contrastingly, many Eastern cultures hold a more positive view of aging. In these societies, older adults are revered for their wisdom and experience. For example, in Japan, there is a national holiday known as Respect for the Aged Day. This day honors elderly citizens, celebrating their longevity and contribution to society. Similarly, in many parts of India, older family members often live with their children and grandchildren, playing significant roles in family decisions and caregiving for younger generations. These cultural practices acknowledge the value and importance of older individuals, contributing to a more positive perception of aging.

One way to positively transform aging perceptions is through intergenerational relationships. When young and old people spend time together, both groups benefit. Older adults can share their knowledge and experiences, while younger people can offer new perspectives and technological skills. These interactions can break down stereotypes and foster mutual respect. Programs that encourage these relationships, like pairing older mentors with young professionals or involving elderly people in schools as volunteer teachers, can help shift negative perceptions and highlight the valuable contributions that older individuals can make.

Education plays a crucial role in changing how aging is viewed. By incorporating lessons about aging into school curricula, children can learn early on about the aging process and the value of older adults. These lessons can cover the biological aspects of aging and also emphasize the social and cultural contributions of older individuals. Education can challenge misconceptions and prepare young people to enter a world where they are likely to live longer and interact with significantly older populations.

Media also has a powerful influence on public perception and can be a tool for positive change. By featuring older adults in diverse roles that go beyond the stereotypical portrayals, media can show that aging is not a decline into insignificance but a stage of life rich with opportunities for continued growth and participation. Films, television shows, and advertisements that depict older individuals as active, happy, and integral parts of society can help reshape public attitudes.

Healthcare systems also have a role in redefining aging. By focusing on preventive care and promoting healthy lifestyles, healthcare providers can help older adults maintain their independence and quality of life for longer. This approach not only benefits the individual but also reduces the burden on healthcare systems by delaying or preventing the chronic diseases commonly associated with old age.

Community planning is another area where changes can lead to improved perceptions of aging. Designing cities and communities with the needs of older adults in mind—such as safe walking paths, ample public transportation options, and accessible public buildings—can help older individuals remain active and engaged in their communities. These designs not only benefit the elderly but improve the community's quality of life for all its members.

Ultimately, redefining aging in a positive way involves valuing the elderly as active, contributing members of society rather than viewing them as passive recipients of care. This shift in perception can lead to more inclusive communities where people of all ages can thrive. As societies around the world grapple with increasing numbers of older adults, transforming how we think about aging is not just beneficial; it is essential. This transformation can ensure that all individuals, regardless of age, are respected and valued for the unique contributions they bring to the world.

ppp

"Aging is not a loss but a new stage of opportunity and strength. It's not about fading away; it's about growing more into ourselves and understanding our true strength."

❦❦❦

TWO

THE JOY OF LIFELONG LEARNING

Lifelong learning is a powerful concept that enriches lives, expanding minds and possibilities, especially as we age. It keeps the mind engaged and the spirit rejuvenated, offering numerous benefits that extend far beyond acquiring new knowledge. Embracing continuous learning can transform the later years into some of the most fulfilling of one's life, providing mental stimulation, opportunities for social interaction, and a profound sense of achievement.

Learning does not stop when formal education ends. On the contrary, it can become even more valuable as one grows older. As we age, the time available for personal development and exploration increases, offering a unique opportunity to dive into new subjects that intrigue us, or deepen our knowledge in areas we've always loved. Whether it's picking up a new musical instrument, learning a new language, or exploring the world of digital photography, each new learning endeavor adds a rich layer to one's sense of self and capacity for growth.

The mental benefits of staying intellectually active are significant. Engaging in learning activities stimulates the brain, helping to keep it sharp and functioning at its best. Studies have shown that mental activity can contribute to a longer cognitive lifespan, potentially delaying the onset of dementia and other age-related cognitive declines. The act of learning challenges the brain, creating new neural pathways and boosting cognitive reserve—the brain's ability to improvise and find alternate ways of completing tasks when challenges arise.

Moreover, lifelong learning also offers substantial emotional benefits. Learning new skills can boost self-confidence and self-esteem, fostering a sense of accomplishment and purpose. This is particularly important in later life as it helps combat feelings of insignificance that may come with retirement or the loss of familial roles. Engaging in educational activities helps older adults feel more connected to contemporary issues and trends, making them feel more relevant in today's fast-paced world.

Socially, lifelong learning creates opportunities to interact with like-minded individuals who share similar interests. Community centers, local colleges, and libraries often offer classes and workshops designed for older adults, providing not only educational but social benefits. Participating in these classes allows individuals to meet new people, perhaps forming friendships that can offer emotional and practical support. This social interaction is crucial as it can decrease feelings of loneliness and isolation, which are common in older age.

In addition, lifelong learning can also be a vehicle for intergenerational interaction, which is mutually beneficial. Older adults can share their knowledge and life experiences with younger generations, providing mentorship and guidance. Conversely, younger people can help older adults stay current with new technologies and trends, such as using smartphones, social media, or understanding the latest in health and wellness.

Economically, the benefits of lifelong learning are equally compelling. In today's economy, retirement is no longer a definitive end to one's career. Many find themselves returning to part-time work or starting new ventures. Lifelong learning can equip older adults with the necessary skills to remain competitive in the job market or to finally start a passion project or business. This not only helps financially but also provides a powerful sense of purpose and community contribution.

Furthermore, the accessibility of learning resources has never been better. The internet offers limitless opportunities for learning, from online university courses to instructional videos on nearly any topic imaginable. Libraries and bookstores are treasure troves of knowledge, often hosting author talks, book clubs, and various classes that can spark new interests or reignite old passions.

Encouraging a lifestyle of continuous learning can therefore transform the perception of aging. Instead of viewing later years as a time of decline, they can be seen as a period of opportunity and growth. With the barriers to education lower than ever before, and the flexibility to learn at one's own pace, older adults are perfectly positioned to take advantage of the benefits offered by lifelong learning.

By maintaining an attitude of curiosity and openness to new experiences, older adults can continue to lead vibrant, intellectually fulfilling lives. This approach not only enriches their own lives but also makes them invaluable members of society, capable of contributing wisdom, stability, and a sense of continuity. Thus, lifelong learning is not just beneficial but essential for anyone looking to lead a rich and rewarding life at any age.

ممم

"*Never let age dim the flame of curiosity. Each day offers us a new opportunity to learn something new, a chance to be surprised and inspired.*"

❥❥❥

THREE
PHYSICAL HEALTH AFTER FIFTY

Maintaining physical health after fifty is vital for enjoying a quality life in later years. As the body ages, physical changes are inevitable, but these changes do not have to diminish one's vitality or zest for life. Staying active and eating well can significantly help maintain strength, flexibility, and energy. This essay explores practical advice on how simple exercises and thoughtful nutrition can support physical health after fifty, ensuring that these years can be some of the best of one's life.

As we age, our muscles naturally begin to lose strength and mass, a process known as sarcopenia. The joints may also show signs of wear and tear, manifesting as stiffness or arthritis. However, these changes can be mitigated through regular physical activity. Exercise is not only crucial for maintaining muscle tone and joint flexibility but also for cardiovascular health, bone density, and overall energy levels.

Starting with exercise, it is essential to incorporate a mix of cardiovascular, strength-training, and flexibility exercises into a weekly routine. Cardiovascular exercises, such as walking, swimming, or cycling, are excellent for heart health and stamina.

They can be easily adjusted to one's fitness level and are generally enjoyable, which increases the likelihood of sticking with them. It is generally recommended to engage in at least 150 minutes of moderate aerobic activity or 75 minutes of vigorous activity per week.

Strength training is equally important after fifty. Lifting weights, using resistance bands, or practicing body-weight exercises like squats, push-ups, and leg raises can help maintain muscle mass and bone density. Strength training also aids in managing weight, as muscle burns more calories than fat, even at rest. It is advisable to include strength training exercises at least two days a week, focusing on all major muscle groups.

Flexibility exercises are often overlooked but are critical to keeping the body agile and preventing injuries. Yoga and stretching are ideal for enhancing flexibility and balance, which can help prevent falls—a common concern for older adults. Incorporating daily stretches or regular yoga sessions can make a significant difference in how limber and energetic one feels.

In addition to exercise, nutrition plays a critical role in maintaining physical health after fifty. As metabolism naturally slows with age, it becomes crucial to focus on nutrient-dense foods that provide the necessary vitamins and minerals without too many excess calories. A balanced diet rich in fruits, vegetables, lean proteins, and whole grains provides the body with the energy needed to sustain an active lifestyle. It is also important to stay hydrated, as older adults may not feel thirsty even when their body needs fluids.

Specific nutrients should receive special attention after fifty. Calcium and vitamin D are essential for bone health, helping prevent osteoporosis. Dairy products, leafy green vegetables, and fortified foods can provide calcium, while vitamin D can be sourced from exposure to sunlight, supplements, and fortified foods.

Omega-3 fatty acids, found in fish, flaxseeds, and walnuts, are important for heart health and cognitive function, which can also be affected by aging.

It is also beneficial to limit the intake of salt, which can contribute to high blood pressure, and sugar, which can lead to weight gain and increase the risk of type 2 diabetes. Instead, focusing on whole foods that are minimally processed can help maintain overall health and energy levels.

Regular medical check-ups are another crucial aspect of maintaining health after fifty. These check-ups can help catch potential health issues early when they are more manageable. Regular screenings for cholesterol levels, blood pressure, and other potential age-related concerns should not be neglected.

Staying socially active and mentally engaged can also contribute to physical health. Participating in social activities, pursuing hobbies, and keeping mentally active through reading, puzzles, or learning can help maintain a healthy mind and body connection.

Maintaining physical health after fifty is fully achievable with regular exercise, proper nutrition, and a proactive approach to healthcare. By incorporating cardiovascular, strength, and flexibility exercises into a regular routine, and by focusing on a nutritious diet, older adults can enjoy increased energy, strength, and flexibility. This proactive approach not only enhances the quality of life but also empowers individuals to live their later years with vitality and joy.

ppp

"Taking care of your body is an investment, not a cost. Treat it well, and it will enable you to experience the world in ways you can only imagine."

❤❤❤

FOUR

Strategies for Fostering Mental Health, Including Mindfulness, Meditation,

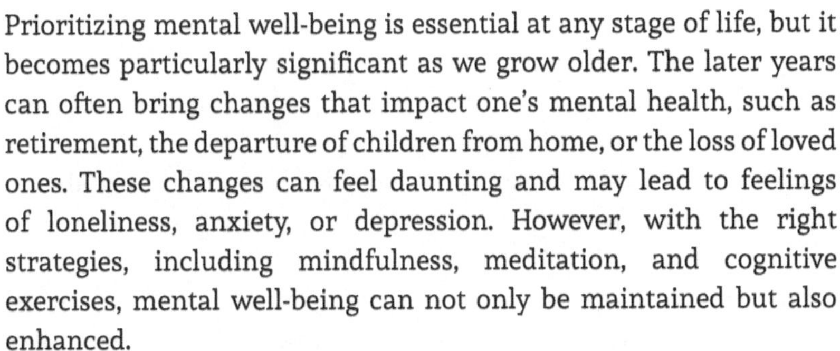

Prioritizing mental well-being is essential at any stage of life, but it becomes particularly significant as we grow older. The later years can often bring changes that impact one's mental health, such as retirement, the departure of children from home, or the loss of loved ones. These changes can feel daunting and may lead to feelings of loneliness, anxiety, or depression. However, with the right strategies, including mindfulness, meditation, and cognitive exercises, mental well-being can not only be maintained but also enhanced.

Mental health is as crucial as physical health, especially after fifty, when the risk of developing mental health issues, such as depression or anxiety, can increase. Engaging regularly in activities that promote mental fitness helps ensure that the mind remains healthy and vigorous. Mindfulness, meditation, and cognitive exercises are powerful tools that can aid in this endeavor, providing both immediate relief from stress and long-term benefits to cognitive function.

Mindfulness involves paying full attention to the present moment without judgment. This practice can be incorporated into daily activities like eating, walking, or even during conversation. By focusing entirely on the here and now, mindfulness helps reduce stress and anxiety. It allows individuals to appreciate life more fully and react to stressful situations more calmly and thoughtfully. Simple ways to practice mindfulness include focusing on one's breath, noticing the sensations of walking, or fully engaging the senses when performing routine tasks. These practices help anchor the mind in the present moment and provide a break from worries about the past or future.

Meditation, often paired with mindfulness, is another effective tool for improving mental well-being. It typically involves sitting quietly and focusing on the breath, a word, or a phrase known as a mantra. Meditation can help decrease stress, lower blood pressure, and improve concentration. It has also been shown to enhance overall happiness and well-being. For those new to meditation, many resources are available, including guided meditations and community classes, which can provide support and instruction. Even a few minutes of meditation each day can make a significant difference in one's mental health.

Cognitive exercises are also essential for maintaining mental sharpness. These can range from puzzles and games like crosswords, Sudoku, and chess to more structured activities like taking a class or learning a new skill. These activities stimulate the brain and can help maintain memory and cognitive function. Engaging regularly in mentally challenging activities has been shown to delay the onset of cognitive decline and can be a fun and rewarding way to keep the mind engaged.

In addition to these practices, social interaction plays a vital role in mental well-being. Maintaining strong social connections can help prevent feelings of loneliness and isolation, which are significant risk factors for mental health issues. Regular interactions with family, friends, or through community groups can provide emotional support and a sense of belonging. Participating in group activities, whether social, educational, or physical, can also contribute positively to mental health.

Physical activity is another critical component of mental well-being. Regular exercise not only helps the body but also has profound benefits for the mind. Physical activity releases endorphins, natural brain chemicals that enhance mood and act as natural painkillers. Exercise also helps regulate sleep, which can significantly affect stress levels and mental health.

Finally, maintaining a routine can provide a sense of structure and purpose, both of which are important for mental health. A daily or weekly routine can include set times for activities such as exercise, socializing, hobbies, and relaxation. This structure helps create a balanced life and can make managing stress easier.

Cultivating mental well-being is an ongoing process that involves mindfulness, meditation, cognitive challenges, social interaction, physical health, and structured routines. By embracing these strategies, individuals can foster a resilient, healthy mind capable of facing the challenges and enjoying the opportunities that come with later years. Prioritizing mental health not only enhances personal happiness and satisfaction but also enriches the lives of those around us, contributing to a more vibrant, supportive community.

❦❦❦

"Cultivate your mind like a garden; good thoughts, like flowers, need attention and care to thrive. Tend to your mental garden, and peace will grow."

FIVE

SOCIAL BUTTERFLIES: STAYING CONNECTED

Staying connected and building new social connections in later years are not just enjoyable aspects of life; they are essential to mental and physical health. Social interactions can significantly enrich one's later years, bringing joy, expanding support networks, and even improving health outcomes. As we age, the importance of social connections often becomes more apparent, especially as life transitions such as retirement or the departure of children create more free time and, potentially, a sense of isolation.

Humans are inherently social beings. From the dawn of civilization, our survival has depended on our ability to form and maintain social groups. This fundamental need does not diminish with age; in fact, maintaining social connections can have even more profound implications as we grow older. Engaging regularly with friends, family, and community members can stave off loneliness, decrease stress, and increase one's sense of belonging and purpose.

One of the key benefits of staying socially active is improved mental health. Social interaction helps keep the mind engaged and sharp. Conversations and social activities stimulate the brain in ways that solitary activities cannot. This stimulation can help delay the onset of dementia and other cognitive declines. Moreover, being part of a social network often means sharing problems and achievements with others, which can significantly reduce feelings of stress and anxiety.

Social connections also contribute to physical health in several direct and indirect ways. People who maintain their social networks as they age tend to have better health than those who are isolated. They are more likely to be physically active, as many social activities involve some level of physical engagement, whether it's walking in a park, attending a dance class, or simply visiting a friend's house. Additionally, people with robust social ties often maintain better dietary habits, as eating is a common social activity. Socially active adults are also less likely to neglect their health since friends and family can encourage medical check-ups and treatment compliance.

Creating and sustaining these connections, however, can require a deliberate effort, especially after major life changes like retirement. One effective way to stay connected is to engage in community activities or volunteer work. These activities not only provide a sense of purpose but also offer opportunities to meet people with similar interests. Many communities offer clubs, classes, and events targeted at older adults, ranging from book clubs and gardening groups to yoga classes and cooking workshops.

Another way to maintain social ties is through technology. The digital world offers incredible opportunities to stay connected with friends and family who may not be physically nearby. Video calls, social media, and messaging apps can bridge vast distances and help maintain relationships. For those less familiar with these technologies, many community centers and libraries offer classes that teach the basics of smartphones, computers, and the internet.

It's also important to be open to forming new relationships. As people age, it's natural to lose connections due to various reasons like relocation, health issues, or even death. Being open to making new friends can help replenish and expand one's social circle. This might mean stepping out of one's comfort zone to talk to strangers or joining new groups, but the benefits of these actions are well worth the effort.

Furthermore, family relationships can play a crucial role in an older adult's social life. Maintaining strong ties with children, grandchildren, and other relatives provides emotional support and strengthens bonds across generations. These relationships can be particularly rewarding, offering love, camaraderie, and mutual support.

Lastly, it's vital for older adults to recognize and combat the common barriers to socializing, such as physical health issues, transportation problems, or even psychological barriers like depression or low self-esteem. Addressing these issues through appropriate medical care, community support, and personal effort is crucial in maintaining an active and fulfilling social life.

Staying socially active and continuing to build new connections are crucial for enriching one's later years. Social interactions provide significant mental and physical health benefits, help combat loneliness, and enhance overall quality of life. By taking proactive steps to stay connected, whether through community involvement, embracing technology, or nurturing family relationships, older adults can enjoy a vibrant, supportive, and healthy social life.

❦❦❦

"Connections with others are the threads that hold the fabric of our lives together. To weave a strong social tapestry, cherish and maintain these bonds."

❤❤❤

SIX

HARNESSING EXPERIENCE

The wealth of wisdom and experience that accumulates over a lifetime is a treasure trove that should not be underestimated. As people age, they gather a vast array of experiences and insights that can not only guide their own decisions but also significantly benefit others around them. Harnessing this experience effectively can lead to a richer, more purposeful life, and can serve as a powerful tool in influencing and educating younger generations, peers, and even societal structures.

The first step in harnessing one's experience is to recognize and value the knowledge gained over the years. This can include professional expertise, life skills, lessons learned from personal relationships, or insights gained from overcoming challenges. Recognizing this accumulated wisdom is not just about reminiscing; it's about understanding the value these experiences hold and how they can be applied in current situations.

One of the most direct ways to utilize this wisdom is through mentorship. Older adults often serve as mentors in professional contexts, where they can guide younger colleagues with the insights they have gained through years of work. But mentorship doesn't have to be confined to professional boundaries. It can also be applied within families, where older family members impart life lessons and values to younger relatives, or within communities, where experienced individuals can offer guidance on everything from gardening to financial planning.

Volunteering is another excellent way for older adults to harness their experience. Many organizations and charities value the insights and reliability that come with seasoned volunteers. Whether it's helping to manage a community garden, contributing to local political campaigns, or leading educational workshops, the opportunities to share knowledge and skills are plentiful and varied.

Teaching is a more formal but incredibly rewarding way to share one's knowledge. Many retirees find joy and purpose in teaching at local schools, community colleges, or through adult education programs. Others might lead seminars or workshops in areas where they hold expertise. Teaching not only allows older adults to pass on their knowledge but also keeps them intellectually engaged and socially active.

Writing is another powerful medium for sharing wisdom. Many people find that writing their memoirs, starting a blog, or contributing articles to magazines or websites about their areas of expertise is a fulfilling way to share their experiences. Writing not only preserves this valuable knowledge for future generations but also provides a reflective space for writers to understand and appreciate their own life journeys.

Besides formal teaching and writing, simply being present and participating in community life can be a way to share wisdom. Participating in community meetings, serving on boards, and being active in local organizations can all be ways in which seasoned individuals can exert influence and guide community decisions.

Their depth of experience can provide historical context and long-term perspectives that might be overlooked by younger members of the community.

On a more personal level, maintaining an active social life and having regular conversations with friends and family can naturally lead to the sharing of valuable insights. These interactions are not only beneficial for those receiving advice but are also enriching for the ones who share, affirming their role and value in their social circles.

In addition to the societal benefits of sharing one's wisdom, there are personal benefits as well. Engaging with others in meaningful ways can combat feelings of loneliness and uselessness that some might feel in later years. It provides a sense of purpose and continuity, reinforcing the idea that one's life experiences are valuable and worth sharing.

The process of harnessing and utilizing experience also encourages a mindset of lifelong learning. In teaching others, individuals often find themselves learning anew, gaining fresh perspectives, and considering alternative viewpoints. This reciprocal exchange of knowledge enhances understanding and fosters a richer, more connected community.

In essence, the act of harnessing experience is a celebration of life's journey. It is a proactive assertion of the ongoing relevance and vitality of older adults in society. By valuing and utilizing the wisdom gained from a lifetime of experiences, older adults not only enrich their own lives but also contribute significantly to the well-being and growth of their communities and beyond.

ᐅᐅᐅ

"Share the wisdom of your years; it is a treasure that increases in value when given away. Your experiences are a roadmap for those who follow."

ᕱᕱᕱ

SEVEN

FINANCIAL FITNESS FOR LATER LIFE

Achieving financial fitness in later life is crucial for ensuring security and peace of mind during retirement. Planning and managing finances wisely can allow one to enjoy the retirement years without the burden of financial stress. Effective financial management after retirement involves budgeting carefully, understanding investment options, managing health care costs, and planning for the unexpected.

The foundation of financial fitness after retirement is budgeting. A detailed and realistic budget is essential to understand how much money is available each month and where it is going. This budget should account for all sources of income, such as pensions, social security benefits, and any income from investments or part-time work. It also needs to cover all expenses, including daily living costs, utilities, home maintenance, transportation, and leisure activities. Prioritizing essential expenses and cutting unnecessary spending are key strategies in maintaining a balanced budget.

It is also important to manage investments wisely. While the approach to investing might change with age, maintaining an investment portfolio can continue to provide necessary income and help protect against inflation. Older adults should consider more conservative investments that provide steady, reliable returns, rather than high-risk investments. However, a mix of investments that includes some growth-oriented assets can also be beneficial, as they offer potential for increased returns. Consulting with a financial advisor who understands the unique needs of retirees can be incredibly helpful in making informed investment decisions.

Another critical aspect of financial fitness in retirement is managing health care costs. Health care can become one of the largest categories of expenses in later life. It is essential to understand the benefits provided by Medicare, as well as any supplementary insurance plans that can cover costs that Medicare does not. Additionally, setting aside a health savings account before retirement can provide tax-advantaged savings that are useful for covering medical expenses incurred during retirement.

Planning for the unexpected is another vital component of financial fitness for retirees. This includes having an emergency fund that can cover unexpected expenses such as home repairs, sudden medical costs, or helping family members in financial need. An emergency fund should be easily accessible and hold enough money to cover several months of living expenses.

Retirees should also consider the potential need for long-term care. The cost of long-term care, whether provided at home or in a facility, can be substantial. Long-term care insurance might be a solution to help manage these costs. This type of insurance typically covers services that regular health insurance or Medicare does not, such as assistance with daily activities and extended nursing care.

Estate planning is another important area that should not be overlooked. This includes setting up wills, trusts, and health care directives. These legal documents ensure that one's wishes are followed in terms of both health decisions and the distribution of assets upon death. Estate planning also helps to minimize the tax burden on heirs and can prevent complicated legal issues and family conflicts.

Furthermore, retirees might find value in continuing to work part-time. Not only can part-time work provide additional income, but it can also offer social interactions and keep one mentally and physically active. Many retirees enjoy consulting, seasonal work, or turning a hobby into a source of income.

Finally, staying educated on financial matters is essential. The world of finance can be complex, and laws and regulations frequently change. Keeping informed through reputable sources can help retirees make better financial decisions and remain aware of any new opportunities or potential challenges.

Achieving financial fitness in later life is multifaceted and requires thoughtful planning and management. By establishing a realistic budget, managing investments wisely, planning for health care costs, preparing for unexpected expenses, considering insurance for long-term care, and conducting thorough estate planning, retirees can ensure financial security and enjoy their later years with peace of mind.

ppp

"Financial health in later life is not about having wealth but managing it wisely. Plan not just for the years you expect, but for the many you have yet to enjoy."

❦❦❦

EIGHT

EMBRACING TECHNOLOGY

Embracing technology can significantly enhance the quality of life, especially in later years. For many older adults, technology may seem daunting due to its rapid pace of change and the perceived complexity of new devices and platforms. However, with a bit of guidance and patience, technology can become a powerful tool for staying connected with loved ones, continuing education, and managing daily activities more efficiently. Here, we explore how older adults can comfortably and effectively integrate technology into their lives.

The first step in embracing technology is overcoming any initial hesitation. It's common for older adults to feel apprehensive about using new technologies, perhaps due to fears of making mistakes or the belief that learning new technologies is too difficult. However, starting with the basics and gradually building skills can demystify technology and increase confidence. Local community centers, libraries, and even some tech stores offer classes designed specifically for seniors. These classes typically cover fundamental skills such as using a smartphone, navigating the internet, setting up email, and understanding social media platforms.

Staying connected with family and friends is one of the most rewarding uses of technology. Social media platforms like Facebook, Instagram, and Twitter allow users to keep up with the lives of their loved ones through photos, videos, and daily updates. Moreover, video calling services such as Skype, Zoom, or FaceTime provide a way to have face-to-face conversations with family and friends, which is particularly valuable for those who live far away from their loved ones. These tools can help alleviate feelings of loneliness and keep older adults socially engaged.

Beyond social media and communication tools, the internet offers vast resources for learning and entertainment. Older adults can use online platforms to enroll in courses covering a wide range of subjects, from history and science to art and music. Websites like Coursera, Udemy, and Khan Academy offer courses taught by experts in the field and are often available for free or at a low cost. Furthermore, technology can reignite past hobbies or help discover new ones; for example, digital photography, online painting tutorials, or even virtual reality experiences that simulate travel to distant places.

Smart devices and apps can also play a crucial role in enhancing daily life by improving convenience and safety. Smartphones can be equipped with apps to track health metrics, such as heart rate or steps walked, which can be shared with healthcare providers. Smart home devices, like smart thermostats, lighting, and security systems, can be controlled remotely, making it easier to manage the home environment efficiently. Additionally, personal assistant devices like Google Home or Amazon Echo can help with setting reminders, playing music, or providing weather updates and news.

Another aspect of technology that can be particularly useful is online banking and shopping. These tools offer the convenience of managing finances and purchasing necessities from the comfort of home. Online banking allows users to check balances, transfer money, pay bills, and more without having to visit a bank. Online shopping can be done on various websites that deliver everything from groceries to medication directly to one's doorstep.

Navigating privacy and security online is also a crucial part of using technology. It is essential for older adults to understand how to protect themselves online by using strong, unique passwords for different sites, enabling two-factor authentication where available, and being cautious about sharing personal information. Learning how to recognize common online scams and fraudulent emails can also help ensure that their experience with technology is safe and positive.

Lastly, the technological landscape is always evolving, and keeping up with new developments can help older adults continue to benefit from the latest tools and resources. Periodically attending refresher courses or workshops can help seniors stay updated on new technologies and trends.

In embracing technology, older adults can find new ways to enhance their lives, from staying connected with family and friends to managing their health and home more effectively. With the right approach and resources, technology can become an empowering tool that offers freedom, convenience, and opportunities for learning and engagement in the digital age.

ϷϷϷ

"Technology is the bridge between generations. Use it to learn, connect, and engage—it's never too late to join the digital conversation."

▷▷▷

NINE

THE ADVENTURE BEGINS AT RETIREMENT

Retirement marks not just an end to a regular working life but the beginning of a new, exciting chapter full of possibilities. It offers an unparalleled opportunity to engage in travel and exploration, activities that can broaden one's horizons and invigorate the spirit. Travel in retirement can be much more than just a leisure activity; it becomes a journey of self-discovery, an educational pursuit, and a source of renewed vitality.

Many people look forward to retirement as the time when they can finally take the trips they've dreamed about for years. Without the constraints of work schedules and with possibly children grown and independent, retirees can explore destinations that have lingered on their bucket lists. Whether it's the romantic streets of Paris, the rugged landscapes of New Zealand, or the historic wonders of Egypt, travel enables retirees to immerse themselves in different cultures, cuisines, and environments.

Traveling in retirement offers numerous benefits, starting with the enhancement of one's mental and physical health. Learning about different cultures, navigating new cities, trying out foreign languages, and meeting new people can provide mental stimulation that keeps the mind sharp. The physical activity involved in exploring new places can also help maintain one's physical health. Even more relaxed trips involve activities that promote physical health, such as walking through museums, hiking in nature reserves, or simply exploring the streets of a bustling city.

Moreover, travel broadens one's perspectives by exposing one to various ways of life, beliefs, and values. This exposure can lead to greater empathy and understanding, breaking down long-held stereotypes and potentially altering viewpoints. It can also provide fresh ideas and inspiration, which can be particularly enriching at a stage in life when one is contemplating life's deeper meanings and new possibilities.

The educational aspects of travel are equally compelling. Retirement travel often includes visits to historical sites, museums, and natural wonders, offering learning experiences that are both engaging and enjoyable. Many retirees take it a step further by participating in organized educational tours that focus on topics such as archaeology, history, or biology. These tours are tailored to provide deeper knowledge and often offer expert guidance that enhances the learning experience.

Additionally, travel in retirement can strengthen existing relationships and forge new ones. Couples often discover new aspects of their relationship while navigating the adventures of travel together. Solo travelers might find camaraderie and friendship in group tours targeted at older adults, where everyone shares a similar zest for exploration. These social interactions are invaluable, providing emotional support and a shared sense of community that can be particularly beneficial in later life.

To embark on these travels, it is important to plan effectively. This involves practical considerations such as budgeting, choosing the right travel insurance, and addressing any health concerns. Budgeting wisely ensures that travel expenses do not strain one's finances, which is crucial in maintaining financial stability in retirement. Travel insurance is more important than ever at this stage of life, as it can cover unexpected health issues or cancellations. Addressing health concerns and ensuring access to necessary medications or medical care while abroad is also essential for a safe and enjoyable trip.

The spirit of adventure doesn't have to lead retirees across the globe; it can also inspire exploration closer to home. Trips to local landmarks, nearby cities, or national parks within one's own country can be just as enriching. These shorter trips can be easier to manage, less expensive, and just as fulfilling, offering the joys of discovery without the stress of long-distance travel.

Retirement opens up a unique phase of life where the freedom to explore becomes a central theme. Travel during this time is not just about seeing new places but about enriching the fabric of one's life. It offers mental and physical benefits, educational opportunities, and the chance to deepen relationships. Whether it's through adventures to distant lands or exploring local treasures, travel can significantly enhance the lives of retirees, providing them with new experiences and memories that will enrich their golden years.

ᖘᖘᖘ

"Travel is the university of life, and lessons are all around us. Every journey is a chance to learn, grow, and see the world through new eyes."

♥♥♥

TEN

VOLUNTEERING: GIVING BACK

Volunteering is a powerful way to give back to the community and enhance one's own life, especially during retirement. Engaging in volunteer work provides numerous benefits, not only for the community but also for the individual volunteer. It enriches personal well-being, fosters social connections, and strengthens community ties. This enriching activity supports personal growth and societal health, making it a beneficial pursuit for individuals of all ages, particularly for those in their retirement years.

One of the primary benefits of volunteering is the positive impact it has on personal well-being. Engaging in volunteer activities can significantly boost mental health by reducing stress, combating depression, and providing a sense of purpose. When individuals volunteer, they contribute to causes they care about, which provides a sense of achievement and fulfillment. The act of helping others leads to increased levels of endorphins, the brain's natural mood elevators, creating a phenomenon often referred to as the "helper's high." Furthermore, volunteering provides a productive way to solve personal problems by offering new perspectives; it can transform an individual's own troubles by immersing them in the service of others who may be facing even greater challenges.

Volunteering also promotes physical health. Studies have shown that those who volunteer have a lower mortality rate than those who do not, even when considering factors like the volunteer's physical health. The activity involved in volunteering—whether it's walking around a local park during a cleanup day, building homes, or even participating in organized walks or runs—can help maintain physical fitness. Additionally, staying active through volunteer work can reduce the risk of chronic diseases associated with aging, including heart disease and hypertension.

Beyond personal health, volunteering strengthens social bonds, which are crucial for emotional support and long-lasting relationships. It offers a platform to meet new people with similar interests, broadening one's social network. This social interaction is particularly beneficial for retirees who might otherwise find their social connections dwindling. Engaging with a community through volunteer activities can alleviate feelings of loneliness and isolation, and provide regular social interaction.

Moreover, volunteering has profound benefits on the health of the community. Volunteers play an essential role in the delivery of charitable services, from helping at food banks and shelters to providing free educational tutoring or health care services. These activities help build stronger communities, bridging gaps between diverse groups and fostering a sense of solidarity and cooperation. Communities with active volunteer participation typically experience fewer social issues, lower crime rates, and better educational outcomes.

Volunteers often bring unique skills and experiences to their roles, which can be especially valuable in community projects. Retired professionals can offer expertise and guidance that might not otherwise be available, contributing to the efficiency and effectiveness of nonprofit organizations. Whether it's a retired teacher tutoring children, a former nurse volunteering at a health clinic, or a business professional helping with fundraising efforts, these contributions can make a significant difference in the operational success of community programs.

In addition to the practical benefits provided, volunteering can also lead to personal growth and development. Volunteers often acquire new skills as they take on various tasks that differ from their previous professional work. These skills can include leadership, teamwork, problem-solving, and communication skills, all of which are transferable to other areas of life. The learning opportunities presented by volunteering can also help keep the mind engaged and active, an important factor in maintaining cognitive health as one ages.

For retirees, volunteering offers a unique opportunity to structure their time and maintain a productive lifestyle. It can provide the routine that work once offered, helping to transition smoothly into the post-retirement phase of life. Furthermore, it allows retirees to pass on valuable knowledge and traditions to younger generations, preserving cultural heritage and fostering community resilience.

Volunteering: Giving Backolunteering is a rewarding activity that benefits both the volunteer and the community. It enhances personal well-being, strengthens social connections, improves physical health, and contributes to community health. For retirees, it offers a meaningful way to give back, stay active, and remain connected, enriching their lives and the lives of others around them. Engaging in volunteer work can transform the golden years into a period of vibrant social activity, continued learning, and profound personal satisfaction.

ϷϷϷ

"Giving back is the heart's way of thanking the world for its gifts. Volunteering weaves your soul into the fabric of the community."

♡♡♡

ELEVEN

THE ART OF HOBBIES

The Art of Hobbies - Exploring new hobbies or revisiting old ones to find joy and possibly discover hidden talents."

Engaging in hobbies is a wonderful way to enrich one's life, offering a source of joy, relaxation, and sometimes even unexpected discoveries about hidden talents. Whether it's taking up new hobbies or revisiting old ones, these activities can provide significant mental and emotional benefits, particularly as we age. Hobbies can range from artistic and creative pursuits to physical and intellectual activities, each offering unique rewards and challenges.

One of the primary benefits of hobbies is the joy and satisfaction they bring. Engaging in activities that one finds enjoyable helps reduce stress and improve mood. Hobbies provide a break from the daily routine, offering a chance to relax and recharge. This mental break can increase productivity and improve one's overall well-being. Moreover, the sense of accomplishment that comes from creating something or improving a skill can boost self-esteem and happiness.

Hobbies also offer an excellent opportunity for social interaction. Many hobbies naturally lead to social engagements, such as knitting clubs, book groups, photography classes, or gardening communities. These settings provide a way to meet new people with similar interests, enhancing one's social life and creating new friendships. For those in retirement or facing significant life changes, these social connections can be particularly valuable, helping to maintain a sense of community and belonging.

Additionally, hobbies can be a great way to maintain mental agility and cognitive function. Engaging in complex activities such as playing a musical instrument, learning a new language, or playing chess can challenge the brain and keep it active. Research has shown that such mentally stimulating activities can help delay the onset of cognitive decline and dementia. Thus, hobbies are not just a way to pass time; they are also a vital part of maintaining mental health.

Exploring new hobbies can also lead to the discovery of hidden talents. Many people may not realize they have a particular skill or aptitude until they try something new. For instance, someone might take up painting on a whim and find that they have a real knack for color and composition. Discovering these hidden talents can be incredibly rewarding and can even lead to new avenues of personal expression and achievement.

Revisiting old hobbies can also be particularly rewarding. Often, hobbies that were set aside due to the demands of work and family responsibilities can be taken up again with a new level of passion and commitment. Returning to these activities can evoke nostalgic feelings and provide a sense of continuity and identity that enhances one's life narrative.

Furthermore, hobbies can adapt to fit one's lifestyle and physical abilities. For instance, someone who enjoyed active sports in their younger years might take up less physically demanding activities such as golf or yoga as they age. This adaptation allows individuals to continue enjoying the benefits of hobbies without strain or injury.

In addition to personal fulfillment, hobbies can also have practical benefits. For example, cooking and gardening not only provide a source of pleasure but also can lead to cost savings and improved health when one is able to cook nutritious meals or grow fresh produce. Similarly, hobbies like woodworking or sewing can produce tangible products that can be used at home or given as gifts, adding an element of utility to the enjoyment they provide.

It is also important to recognize that engaging in hobbies can sometimes turn into more than just a pastime. What starts as a hobby can evolve into a second career or a volunteer opportunity. For example, a hobby photographer might start a small business selling their photographs, or a gardening enthusiast might volunteer at a community garden, sharing their skills and knowledge with others.

Hobbies offer a range of benefits that can significantly enhance one's life. They provide joy, social interaction, mental stimulation, and sometimes even physical benefits. Whether exploring new hobbies or revisiting old ones, these activities can lead to personal growth, discovery of hidden talents, and even new opportunities. For anyone looking to enrich their life, especially those in later stages, hobbies are a key ingredient to a happier, healthier, and more fulfilling life.

ppp

"Hobbies are our private passions, the pursuits that
recharge our spirits and remind us who we are.
Dive into your interests and let joy overflow."

❥❥❥

TWELVE
MINDSET MATTERS

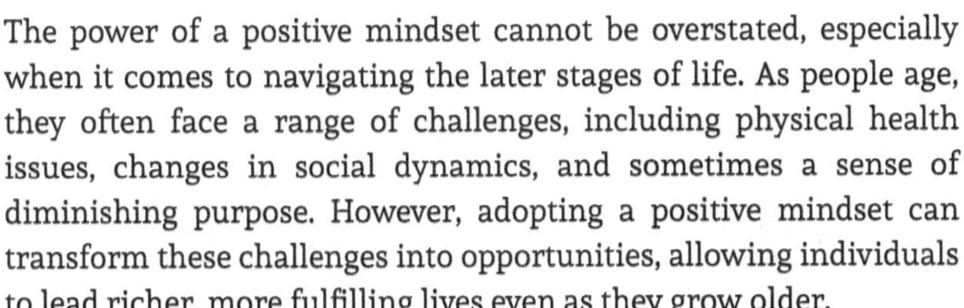

The power of a positive mindset cannot be overstated, especially when it comes to navigating the later stages of life. As people age, they often face a range of challenges, including physical health issues, changes in social dynamics, and sometimes a sense of diminishing purpose. However, adopting a positive mindset can transform these challenges into opportunities, allowing individuals to lead richer, more fulfilling lives even as they grow older.

A positive mindset begins with the recognition that aging is a natural part of life, characterized not just by decline but also by growth and new possibilities. By focusing on the opportunities that aging provides, such as more free time, wisdom gained from life experiences, and the freedom to pursue long-held interests, older adults can approach this stage of life with enthusiasm and optimism.

One of the critical aspects of maintaining a positive mindset is gratitude. Gratitude involves appreciating the good things in life, which can become especially important in later years. Focusing on what one is grateful for—be it family, friends, health, or accomplishments—can significantly boost mood and overall well-being. Studies have shown that people who practice gratitude regularly report fewer health problems and less depression, and they even tend to live longer.

Moreover, a positive mindset influences physical health. Optimism has been linked to better immune function, lower stress levels, and lower risk of cardiovascular disease. Optimistic individuals tend to adopt healthier behaviors, such as regular physical activity, a balanced diet, and adequate sleep, all of which are crucial for aging well. They are also more likely to engage in proactive health behaviors like regular check-ups and following medical advice.

Resilience plays a vital role in cultivating a positive mindset. Aging inevitably brings various losses and changes, but resilience allows individuals to recover from setbacks and adapt to new circumstances. Resilient people view challenges as opportunities for growth and learning, rather than insurmountable obstacles. Developing resilience can involve maintaining strong social networks, keeping a sense of humor, and practicing adaptive coping strategies, such as mindfulness and relaxation techniques.

Furthermore, a positive mindset helps in nurturing social connections, which are incredibly important in later life. People who approach social interactions with positivity and openness are more likely to build and maintain relationships. These connections provide emotional support, intellectual stimulation, and opportunities for meaningful engagement. Socially connected individuals typically report higher levels of life satisfaction and lower levels of mental health issues like depression and anxiety.

Embracing a positive mindset also encourages lifelong learning, which can be particularly enriching during the later years. With more time available, retirees can explore new interests or deepen existing passions. Whether it's taking up a new hobby, learning a new language, or attending lectures and workshops, continuous learning keeps the mind active and engaged, contributing to cognitive health.

Moreover, a positive mindset enhances one's sense of purpose. Many people find that with aging comes a shift in priorities, with an increased focus on personal fulfillment, relationships, and the legacy they wish to leave. By focusing on these aspects, individuals can find new meaning and direction in their lives, countering any feelings of loss that might come with retiring from a career or experiencing other life transitions.

Adopting a positive mindset is not merely about being happy—it is a comprehensive approach to life that involves gratitude, resilience, proactive health behaviors, and an openness to new experiences. By seeing the challenges of aging as opportunities, individuals can transform their later years into one of the most vibrant and rewarding phases of their lives. A positive mindset is thus not just beneficial but essential for anyone looking to navigate the complexities of aging with grace and vitality.

ႣႣႣ

"The mind is powerful—shape it with positivity, and life will respond in kind. View each challenge as an opportunity to grow and thrive."

❦❦❦

THIRTEEN

HOME SWEET HOME

Adapting one's living space to meet evolving needs is a crucial aspect of maintaining independence and comfort, especially as we age. The home environment plays a significant role in our daily lives, influencing our safety, well-being, and ability to perform everyday activities. As physical capabilities change, modifying the home can help ensure that it remains a safe, comfortable, and supportive space. This essay explores practical tips for adapting living spaces to meet the needs of older adults, ensuring they can continue to live independently and comfortably.

Firstly, safety is paramount when considering adaptations to the home. As mobility decreases with age, the risk of falls can increase. To address this, removing tripping hazards is essential. This includes securing or removing loose rugs, decluttering walkways, and ensuring that cables and wires are not strewn across the floor. Adding non-slip mats in areas prone to wetness, such as the bathroom and kitchen, can also prevent slips.

Proper lighting is another critical factor in home safety. Adequate lighting helps prevent falls and makes it easier to perform daily tasks, especially as eyesight diminishes with age. Installing brighter, more energy-efficient lights and ensuring that all areas of the home are well-lit can make a significant difference. This includes hallways, staircases, and closets, where poor lighting can lead to accidents.

Accessibility can be enhanced by making structural modifications to the home. For those who find stairs challenging, installing a stairlift or moving the bedroom and bathroom to the first floor can be beneficial. For wheelchair users or those who rely on walkers, widening doorways and installing ramps instead of steps at entrances can improve mobility within the home.

The bathroom deserves special attention because it is a common site for falls due to its slippery surfaces. Installing grab bars in the shower, beside the toilet, and near the bathtub can provide support and help prevent accidents. Consider a walk-in shower or tub, which eliminates the need to step over a high threshold, and add a shower seat and adjustable showerhead for added comfort and safety.

The kitchen is another area where practical modifications can enhance independence. Lowering countertops and the sink can make them more accessible to those in wheelchairs or with limited reach. Replacing knobs on cabinets and drawers with pull handles can make them easier to open, and installing a pull-out pantry can improve access to food items and kitchen tools.

Furniture placement and choice also play a vital role in adapting a home for older adults. Furniture should be sturdy and easy to use, with chairs and sofas that have firm, high seats to facilitate easier standing and sitting. Ensuring that there is ample space around furniture to move freely, particularly with mobility aids, is essential.

Smart home technology can also significantly enhance the comfort and safety of a home for older adults. Automated systems that control lighting, temperature, and security can be operated remotely, making it easier to manage the home environment. Voice-activated devices can help perform tasks like turning off lights or making phone calls without the need to move around.

Regular maintenance is crucial to keeping the home safe and functional. This includes checking that all appliances are in good working order, ensuring that heating and cooling systems are serviced regularly, and keeping all walkways and driveways clear of snow, leaves, or other debris.

Finally, considering future needs when making home adaptations is important. While current needs might be met with minor adjustments, thinking ahead can prevent the need for more significant changes later on. For example, when renovating, choosing designs and products that are age-friendly can save time, effort, and expense in the future.

Adapting your home to suit changing needs as you age is a proactive approach to maintaining independence and comfort. By focusing on safety, accessibility, and usability, you can create a living space that supports your lifestyle and allows you to enjoy your home for many years to come. These adaptations not only enhance the quality of daily living but also provide peace of mind, knowing that the home environment is secure and supportive.

▷▷▷

"Our homes should evolve as we do, adapting to our
needs and comforting our spirits. Make your space
a haven that mirrors your life's journey."

❦❦❦

FOURTEEN

NAVIGATING HEALTH CARE

Navigating the health care system as we age is essential for maintaining good health, managing chronic conditions, and ensuring that medical care is timely, effective, and affordable. Understanding the intricacies of the health care system can be daunting, but with the right knowledge and strategies, it's possible to make the system work to your advantage, enhancing your well-being and quality of life during your senior years.

The first step in effectively navigating the health care system is to educate yourself about the different types of health care coverage and what they entail. For many older adults, this includes Medicare, Medicaid, and possibly supplemental insurance plans. Medicare, a federal program for those age 65 and older, includes several parts: Part A for hospital insurance, Part B for medical insurance, Part D for prescription drug coverage, and Medicare Advantage plans that offer additional benefits. Understanding the benefits and limitations of each part, as well as when and how to enroll, is crucial. For those with low income and limited resources, Medicaid can provide additional health coverage, and understanding how to qualify and apply is important.

It's also beneficial to understand the health care providers and services available within your insurance network. Knowing which doctors, hospitals, and specialists are covered by your insurance plan can prevent unexpected expenses and ensure you receive care from providers who meet your health needs. Furthermore, it's important to understand the referral and pre-authorization processes that your insurance may require for visiting specialists or obtaining certain tests or procedures.

Effective communication with health care providers is another critical aspect of navigating the health care system. It's important to be prepared for medical appointments with a list of questions or concerns. Keeping a written record of your medical history, including previous illnesses, surgeries, and medications, along with documenting your symptoms and questions, can improve the quality of communication with your health care provider. Being open and honest about your health concerns and lifestyle can help your doctor make better-informed decisions about your care.

Managing medications is a key component of managing health as you age. This includes understanding what each medication is for, how to take it properly, and being aware of potential side effects or interactions with other medications. Using a single pharmacy can help as pharmacists can oversee your medication list and catch potential interactions. Regularly reviewing your medications with your healthcare provider or pharmacist is important to ensure all medications are still necessary and working effectively.

Another essential element is preventative care. Regular check-ups, screenings, and vaccinations can prevent diseases or detect them early when they are most treatable. It's important to know what screenings are recommended for your age group and health condition, such as blood pressure screenings, cholesterol checks, diabetes checks, and cancer screenings.

As you age, it might also be necessary to coordinate among various health care professionals, especially if you have multiple health conditions. This can include regular doctors, specialists, physical therapists, and more. Ensuring that all your health providers are informed about all aspects of your health and treatments can improve your care and avoid unnecessary or conflicting treatments.

Understanding your rights as a patient is also critical. This includes knowing how to access medical records, understanding patient confidentiality laws, and knowing how to file complaints if you're not satisfied with your care. Being informed about these rights can empower you to make decisions about your health care and to advocate for yourself in the health care system.

Finally, planning for future health care needs, including long-term care, is important. This might involve looking into long-term care insurance, learning about assisted living and nursing home options, and considering the designation of a healthcare power of attorney. Preparing for these decisions ahead of time can ease the burden when more intensive levels of care are needed.

Effectively navigating the health care system requires knowledge, communication, and proactive management of your health care needs. By understanding your health insurance coverage, effectively communicating with your health care providers, managing your medications, and utilizing preventative care, you can make the health care system work more effectively for you as you age. This proactive approach not only helps in maintaining good health but also ensures that the care received is aligned with your personal health goals and needs.

ᎮᎮᎮ

*"Understanding health care is key to empowerment.
Take charge of your health decisions, and make the
system work for you, not against you."*

♥♥♥

FIFTEEN

THE LEGACY WE LEAVE

When we think about the concept of a legacy, it often brings to mind what we leave behind for others when we're gone. This can encompass material assets, but, more profoundly, it includes the memories, values, and influences we impart. Shaping a meaningful legacy is an integral part of our lives, reflecting our deepest values and the impact we wish to have on the world. It's about the mark we leave on our families, communities, and, possibly, on a broader scale. Here we explore how anyone can shape a positive and impactful legacy through thoughtful actions and deliberate choices.

First, consider the values you cherish most and wish to pass on. These might include kindness, diligence, creativity, or resilience. Demonstrating these values in daily life is the simplest yet most powerful way to establish a legacy. For example, if kindness is a core value, regularly engaging in acts of kindness—from helping a neighbour to volunteering—can instill this value in those around you, potentially rippling out to affect others you may never meet.

Family often plays a pivotal role in our legacy. Many people think of their children and grandchildren as primary bearers of their legacy. Sharing stories, spending quality time together, and teaching skills or lessons that have significant personal meaning can profoundly impact young family members. Moreover, writing letters or creating video recordings discussing life lessons, personal histories, and hopes for the future can be treasured by younger generations for years to come.

Community involvement is another avenue through which one can build a legacy. By contributing to the betterment of your community—whether through service, leadership, or participation in community events—you leave a footprint that can outlast your direct involvement. Initiatives like planting a community garden, leading a local group, or organizing charity events can create lasting benefits that will be remembered as part of your legacy.

Professional life also offers a platform for legacy building. The impact made through one's career—whether it's inspiring colleagues, mentoring newcomers, or innovating in your field—can form a significant part of how you are remembered. Sharing your expertise, dedicating time to mentor others, and striving to make ethical, forward-thinking business decisions can influence many and create a professional legacy based on respect and inspiration.

Writing and creative expressions provide a tangible means of shaping a legacy. Many choose to write memoirs, essays, or books that articulate their life experiences, wisdom, and values. Others might express their legacy through art, music, or craft, leaving behind creations that speak to future generations. These works can communicate personal narratives and insights that resonate and inspire long into the future.

Philanthropy is another powerful tool for legacy building. By supporting causes and organizations that align with your values, you can make a lasting impact that extends beyond your immediate reach. Setting up scholarships, contributing to charities, and funding projects that drive social change can all be part of a philanthropic legacy that continues to benefit others.

Finally, consider the emotional legacy left through everyday interactions. The way you treat people, the kindness and respect you show, and the encouragement you give can profoundly impact others' lives. These interactions might not always be remembered individually but will shape the general memory of your character and how you made others feel.

Shaping a legacy is not solely about material possessions but rather about the impact of your actions and choices throughout your life. Whether through family, community, professional endeavours, creative outputs, philanthropy, or simple daily interactions, the legacy we leave can influence others and the world in profound and lasting ways. Taking deliberate steps to embody your values and share your insights ensures that the legacy you leave is one that truly reflects who you are and what you believe in, making a lasting difference in the lives of others.

ppp

"What we leave behind is not engraved on
monuments, but woven into the lives of others.
Cultivate a legacy that makes waves for
generations to come."

ppp

SIXTEEN

FASHION AND SELF-EXPRESSION AFTER FIFTY

Fashion and self-expression are not confined to the young. As we age, maintaining a vibrant and evolving personal style can significantly enhance our sense of identity and self-esteem. Fashion after fifty is not just about adhering to trends; it's about expressing who you are and feeling great in your own skin. This essay explores how individuals over fifty can keep their personal style dynamic and reflective of their personality, continuing to evolve with fashion while remaining true to what best suits their lifestyle and preferences.

Firstly, it's essential to recognize that personal style is an extension of oneself. As people age, they often become more confident in their skin and have a clearer understanding of what they like and dislike. This confidence should be mirrored in their wardrobe choices. Style after fifty should be about celebrating individuality and feeling good about one's appearance. Embracing colors that you love, styles that flatter your body shape, and patterns that speak to your personal aesthetic are all ways to enhance your wardrobe and reflect your personality.

One important aspect to consider is the changing nature of one's body. As we age, our body shapes can change, and it might become necessary to adjust our fashion choices accordingly. This doesn't mean resorting to less stylish clothing but rather finding cuts and styles that enhance your current body shape. Tailored clothing can be incredibly flattering; well-fitting pieces can accentuate your best features and make you feel more confident. Investing in a few key pieces that fit well and make you feel comfortable can make a significant difference in your wardrobe and daily comfort.

Accessorizing is another effective way to express individual style. Accessories like jewelry, scarves, hats, and glasses can transform a simple outfit into something special and are an easy way to reflect personality without altering an entire wardrobe. Accessories can also be a form of playful expression, offering the flexibility to change with trends without significant investment or commitment.

Staying updated with fashion trends can also inspire and rejuvenate your personal style. However, staying trendy doesn't mean one must adopt every new fashion that comes along. Instead, it's about selecting elements of current trends that resonate with your personal style and integrating them into your wardrobe in a way that feels authentic. For instance, you might incorporate a trendy color or a contemporary style of shoe into your classic wardrobe to refresh your look without overhauling it entirely.

Moreover, comfort does not have to be sacrificed for style. The market for stylish, comfortable clothing has expanded, with many brands now focusing on creating garments that look great and are easy to wear. Fabrics that stretch and provide comfort throughout the day are essential for maintaining an active lifestyle without compromising on style.

Another key to evolving fashion and self-expression after fifty is to maintain an adventurous spirit towards fashion. Trying new styles or revisiting styles you once loved but set aside can be refreshing. Fashion should be fun and a form of personal expression, regardless of age.

Furthermore, self-expression through fashion can also be an opportunity to connect with others. Sharing fashion tips with friends, shopping together, or discussing style ideas can be a way to enhance social interactions and enjoy fashion as a shared interest.

Maintaining a vibrant and evolving personal style after fifty is about embracing your identity, understanding and adapting to body changes, and being selective with trends to suit your personal taste. It involves mixing comfort with style, using accessories to enhance outfits, and keeping an open mind to new fashion ideas. Above all, fashion at any age is about feeling confident and expressing yourself in ways that make you feel happiest and most at ease.

❦❦❦

"Dress not for the years in your life, but for the life in your years. Fashion is about expressing your inner self, not following someone else's trend."

❥❥❥

SEVENTEEN
NUTRITION FOR LONGEVITY

Nutrition plays a critical role in promoting long-term health and vitality, especially as we age. A well-balanced diet can help prevent chronic diseases, maintain energy levels, and support overall well-being. This essay explores the key components of nutrition that are essential for longevity, offering insights into foods and diet plans that can help individuals lead a healthier and more vibrant life after fifty.

The foundation of a diet for longevity is built on whole, nutrient-dense foods. These include a variety of fruits and vegetables, whole grains, lean proteins, and healthy fats. Each of these food groups provides unique nutrients that are essential for maintaining health and preventing age-related decline.

Fruits and vegetables are rich in vitamins, minerals, fiber, and antioxidants, which are substances that protect the body from oxidative stress and inflammation, two processes that contribute to aging and chronic disease. Including a variety of colors in your diet is a useful way to ensure you're getting a broad range of these nutrients. For example, dark leafy greens like spinach and kale are high in vitamins A, C, and K, while berries are loaded with antioxidants known for their brain-health benefits.

Whole grains provide an important source of fiber, which is crucial for digestive health and maintaining a healthy weight. Fiber helps keep the digestive system running smoothly and can lower the risk of diseases such as type 2 diabetes and heart disease. Whole grains like quinoa, barley, and whole wheat also offer essential vitamins and minerals needed for cellular health and energy.

Protein is vital for muscle repair, bone health, and maintaining muscle mass, which naturally declines with age. Including a variety of protein sources, such as lean meats, fish, eggs, and plant-based options like beans and lentils, ensures you get a full range of essential amino acids. Fish such as salmon and mackerel are particularly beneficial because they are high in omega-3 fatty acids, which are important for heart and brain health.

Healthy fats are also crucial for longevity. These fats, found in foods like nuts, seeds, avocados, and olive oil, support brain function, reduce inflammation, and help maintain healthy skin and joints. Incorporating these fats into your diet instead of saturated fats found in butter and fatty meats can help improve cholesterol levels and protect against heart disease.

Hydration is another critical element of a healthy diet, especially for older adults, who may not feel thirsty as often as younger people. Drinking sufficient water is vital for kidney function, digestion, and skin health. Herbal teas and water-rich foods like cucumbers and melons can also contribute to overall hydration.

Beyond individual foods, certain dietary patterns have been linked to longevity and reduced risk of chronic diseases. The Mediterranean diet is one such pattern, well-known for its emphasis on whole grains, fresh fruits and vegetables, fish, olive oil, and moderate wine consumption. This diet has been associated with a lower risk of heart disease and improved lifespan.

Another aspect of nutrition for longevity involves mindful eating—paying attention to what, when, and how much you eat. Listening to your body's hunger cues and eating meals without distractions can help regulate food intake and enhance the enjoyment of meals. This practice supports a healthy relationship with food and helps prevent overeating, which is crucial for maintaining a healthy weight.

Finally, it's important to adapt your diet to any specific health needs you may have as you age, such as adjusting sodium intake for blood pressure management or increasing calcium and vitamin D for bone health. Regular consultations with a healthcare provider or a nutritionist can help tailor your eating habits to these needs.

Embracing a diet rich in diverse, nutrient-dense foods is key to promoting longevity and vitality. By focusing on whole foods, balanced nutrients, and healthy eating patterns, and by adapting to changing health needs, individuals can greatly influence their health outcomes positively. This approach not only contributes to a longer life but also ensures that the years lived are vibrant and fulfilling.

ppp

"Eat not just to fill your stomach but to nourish your soul. Good food supports the body, sharpens the mind, and heals the heart."

♥♥♥

EIGHTEEN
STAYING SAFE

Staying safe and secure is a crucial concern for everyone, but it becomes particularly important as we age. In the later years, the challenges to safety can increase both physically and online. Ensuring personal safety involves a comprehensive approach that includes safeguarding oneself from physical dangers as well as protecting against online threats. This essay will provide practical tips and strategies for maintaining safety and security in later life, encompassing both the physical and digital realms.

Physical Safety

One of the primary concerns for older adults is physical safety at home, where most accidents occur, particularly falls. To minimize the risk of falls, it's essential to maintain a clutter-free environment. Removing loose carpets, securing electrical cords, and ensuring that walkways both inside and outside the home are clear can significantly reduce fall risks. Adequate lighting is also crucial. Installing brighter bulbs and ensuring that areas like stairways and bathrooms are well-lit can prevent accidents that occur due to poor visibility.

Bathrooms require special attention as they are common sites for falls. Installing grab bars in the shower, near the toilet, and in other strategic areas of the bathroom can provide stability and support. Non-slip mats in the shower and on the bathroom floor are also highly recommended to prevent slips on wet surfaces.

In terms of home security, older adults should ensure that their homes are equipped with sturdy locks on all doors and windows. A peephole or a security camera can add an extra layer of protection, allowing individuals to see who is at the door without opening it. Additionally, having a list of emergency contacts easily accessible in multiple locations throughout the home, along with a phone within reach, can provide a sense of security in case of emergencies.

Road Safety

For those who continue to drive, road safety is another important consideration. Regular vision and hearing tests are crucial as these senses tend to decline with age and can significantly impact driving abilities. It's also wise to avoid driving in adverse conditions such as during heavy rain, at night, or in heavy traffic areas when possible. Attending refresher driving courses can help older adults stay up-to-date with road rules and improve driving skills.

Community Safety

Engaging with the community can also enhance personal safety. Participating in local neighborhood watch programs or community groups can keep one informed about local safety issues and strengthen community ties, which can be a source of support in times of need.

Online Safety

As more older adults are using the internet, online safety has become increasingly significant. Protecting oneself online involves understanding the risks and knowing how to deal with them effectively. One of the simplest yet most effective steps is to use strong, unique passwords for different online accounts and change them regularly. Using a password manager can help keep track of various passwords securely.

Being aware of common online scams targeting older adults is also crucial. This includes phishing attempts, where scammers impersonate legitimate companies or organizations to steal personal information. Being cautious about sharing any personal or financial information over the internet and verifying the authenticity of requests by contacting organizations directly through official channels can prevent most of these scams.

Installing reputable antivirus software and keeping it updated can protect against malware and other malicious threats. It's also important to keep software up-to-date, as updates often include security enhancements.

Social Media and Privacy

For those who use social media, adjusting privacy settings to control who can see your information and posts is vital. Be wary of friend requests from strangers and think carefully before sharing personal information, such as your home address or current location, online.

Staying safe in later years requires a multi-faceted approach that encompasses physical safety measures, vigilant driving practices, community engagement, and robust online security. By taking proactive steps to address these areas, older adults can protect their well-being and continue to live independently and confidently. Understanding and implementing these safety measures can greatly enhance the quality of life, ensuring that the golden years are not only joyful but also secure.

ppp

"Safety isn't just locking doors; it's safeguarding your independence. Be vigilant, be smart, and protect the life you've worked so hard to build."

♥♥♥

NINETEEN

INTERGENERATIONAL BONDS

Fostering intergenerational bonds is a deeply enriching practice that offers significant benefits, not just to older adults but to younger generations as well. These relationships, bridging the gap between different age groups, can enhance mutual understanding, provide educational opportunities, and enrich the lives of all involved. By connecting more frequently and meaningfully with younger people, older adults can experience renewed vitality, impart wisdom, and create a legacy of knowledge and values that can guide the younger generations.

One of the fundamental benefits of intergenerational relationships is the exchange of knowledge. Older adults possess a wealth of experience and insights that can be invaluable to younger people. Whether it's practical life skills, professional advice, or historical knowledge, older generations have much to teach. Conversely, younger people often bring fresh perspectives and are usually more attuned to new technologies and cultural shifts. This exchange can stimulate learning on both sides, with older adults keeping up more effectively with societal changes and young people gaining a deeper understanding of their cultural and historical roots.

These relationships also offer emotional benefits. For older adults, engaging with the younger generation can help alleviate feelings of isolation or loneliness, which are common in later life. Being around younger people can be energizing and invigorating, often leading to a more active and engaged lifestyle. For children and young adults, interactions with elders can provide emotional stability and a sense of continuity. This is particularly valuable in today's often transient society, where extended families might not always live close together.

Intergenerational connections can also help to address and dispel common stereotypes. Younger individuals might hold misconceptions about aging, seeing it only as a period of decline, while older adults may feel out of touch with younger people, viewing them as disengaged or overly dependent on technology. Through regular interaction, both groups can break down these stereotypes. Young people can learn to appreciate the capabilities and the contributions of the elderly, and older adults can gain a more positive view of the younger generation's potential and values.

Mentorship is a powerful aspect of intergenerational relationships. Many older adults find a renewed sense of purpose in mentoring young people. They can guide them through academic, professional, or personal challenges, benefiting from the fulfillment of impacting someone else's life positively. For young people, having a mentor means having a supportive guide—a person who provides not only knowledge but also emotional support and wisdom.

Furthermore, these relationships can strengthen community bonds. When different generations engage regularly, it fosters a sense of belonging and community spirit. Communities that encourage such engagement tend to be more cohesive, with lower levels of age-related segregation and a stronger communal identity. Programs that promote intergenerational interaction, like community centers or local events that involve multiple age groups, can enhance these community bonds.

Family dynamics also benefit greatly from strong intergenerational bonds. In families where children, parents, and grandparents frequently interact, there is often an increased sense of family unity and support. Grandparents, in particular, can play a unique role in family life, providing care, wisdom, and a link to family heritage. In return, older adults often report higher levels of life satisfaction and a greater sense of well-being when they have close relationships with their grandchildren.

In practical terms, fostering these bonds can involve regular family gatherings, shared hobbies or projects, or structured programs like tutoring or storytelling sessions where older adults interact with younger people. Technology can also bridge generational gaps; teaching a grandparent to use social media or video calling can open new channels of communication and shared experiences.

Intergenerational relationships are not only beneficial but essential for a healthy, vibrant society. They provide educational and emotional benefits, reduce stereotypes, offer mentorship opportunities, and strengthen community ties. By investing in these relationships, both young and old can share in the rich, reciprocal benefits of a connected, intergenerational community, enriching their lives and the broader social fabric.

ᑭᑭᑭ

"*The wisdom of the old and the energy of the young
are society's greatest assets. When combined, they
create a force more powerful than either alone.*"

❥❥❥

TWENTY
CELEBRATING MILESTONES

Celebrating milestones is a fundamental aspect of life that offers us a chance to reflect, appreciate, and commemorate the significant events and transitions we experience. These celebrations can help us to acknowledge our achievements, honour our journeys, and maintain traditions that connect us with our cultural or family heritage. From birthdays and anniversaries to retirements and memorials, each milestone can be marked in meaningful ways that resonate personally and collectively, fostering a sense of continuity and joy at every stage of life.

Birthdays are perhaps the most commonly celebrated personal milestones. They are a celebration of life and an annual occasion to reflect on the past year while looking forward to the future. As people age, these celebrations can shift from lavish parties to more intimate gatherings with close family and friends. For significant birthdays such as the 50th, 60th, or 75th, some may choose to organize larger events, bringing together extended family and friends to mark the occasion in a special way. Sharing stories, reminiscing about past events, and expressing hopes for the future are meaningful ways to celebrate these important birthdays.

Anniversaries, especially those marking significant numbers of years, are another cornerstone for celebration. They provide an opportunity for couples to renew their commitment to each other and reflect on the growth and bonds they have shared. Celebrating anniversaries might involve a special dinner, a vow renewal ceremony, or a getaway to a place significant to the couple. It's also a chance for family and friends to honor the couple's journey, offering gifts, cards, or organizing a surprise party that shows appreciation and love.

Graduations mark important educational milestones and signify the transition from one phase of life to another. These are times of great pride and are often celebrated with ceremonies and parties. As individuals move from school to higher education or from university to the workforce, these milestones underscore their hard work and aspirations. Celebrating these achievements can involve throwing a party, gathering family for a dinner, or giving thoughtful gifts that prepare them for their next steps, such as books, technology, or professional attire.

Retirements are significant milestones that mark the end of a long career and the beginning of a new chapter of life. A retirement party can be a joyful, poignant event that offers colleagues, friends, and family a chance to celebrate the retiree's contributions and achievements. Such celebrations might include speeches, presentations, or slideshow recaps of the retiree's career, highlighting significant moments and achievements. Gifts that reflect the retiree's hobbies or plans for retirement are also thoughtful ways to mark this transition.

Memorial milestones, such as the anniversary of a loved one's passing, are solemn yet important occasions that deserve recognition. These might be marked by gathering family and friends to share memories, visiting the loved one's resting place, or performing acts of charity in their memory. Such events help families and friends find closure, honor memory, and process grief in a supportive setting.

In addition to these common milestones, there are numerous cultural and religious milestones that vary widely between different communities and traditions. These can include rites of passage such as bar or bat mitzvahs, quinceañeras, first communions, or other ceremonies that signify important religious or cultural transitions. Celebrating these milestones in traditional ways can help preserve cultural heritage and strengthen community bonds.

Seasonal milestones such as anniversaries of home ownership or the start of a new season can also be moments of celebration. These might be marked by annual parties, family gatherings, or community festivals. Such celebrations can turn into cherished annual traditions that build a sense of belonging and continuity.

Practical Tips for Celebrating Milestones:

Plan ahead: Give yourself enough time to organize the event, invite guests, and manage logistics.

Personalize: Tailor the celebration to reflect the preferences and personality of the honoree.

Document the occasion: Take photos or videos, keep a guest book, or encourage guests to share stories and messages.

Include everyone: Especially for significant events, consider ways to include distant family and friends, possibly through virtual means.

Celebrating milestones is a vital part of life that enhances our sense of community, continuity, and personal identity. Whether through large gatherings or quiet reflections, marking these moments helps commemorate our past, celebrate our present, and inspire our future. By acknowledging and cherishing each significant event, we weave the rich tapestry of our lives, filled with memories and meaning that last a lifetime.

ᚦᚦᚦ

"Every milestone is a reflection of the path we've traveled. Celebrate each as a victory, a moment of reflection, and a stepping stone to further adventures."

ᗠᗠᗠ

TWENTY-ONE
SUMMARY

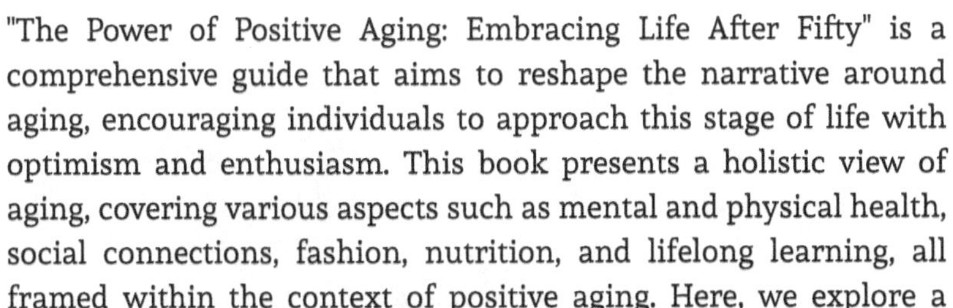

"The Power of Positive Aging: Embracing Life After Fifty" is a comprehensive guide that aims to reshape the narrative around aging, encouraging individuals to approach this stage of life with optimism and enthusiasm. This book presents a holistic view of aging, covering various aspects such as mental and physical health, social connections, fashion, nutrition, and lifelong learning, all framed within the context of positive aging. Here, we explore a summary of the key themes and advice presented in the book, drawing together insights from each chapter to offer a cohesive blueprint for thriving in later years.

Redefining Aging: The book begins by challenging the conventional views of aging, promoting a shift in perception that sees aging not as a decline but as a period of opportunity and growth. It discusses how different cultures view aging and suggests ways to adopt more positive attitudes that recognize the contributions and value of older adults.

Lifelong Learning: Emphasizing the importance of continual mental engagement, the book encourages older adults to pursue new educational avenues that keep their minds active. Whether through formal classes, reading, or hobbies, lifelong learning is presented as a key to maintaining cognitive health and staying connected with contemporary issues.

Physical Health: Maintaining physical health is crucial for enjoying later life. The book provides practical advice on integrating routine physical activity and proper nutrition to combat common health issues associated with aging. It also emphasizes the importance of regular medical check-ups and being proactive in managing one's health.

Mental Well-being: Mental health gets a spotlight with discussions on the benefits of mindfulness, meditation, and positive thinking. The book offers strategies to foster mental well-being, such as engaging in social activities, practicing gratitude, and finding ways to stay involved in community life.

Social Connections: Highlighting the importance of maintaining and building new social relationships, the book explains how social interactions can enhance one's quality of life, reduce feelings of loneliness, and provide emotional support during the aging process.

Harnessing Experience: Older adults are encouraged to leverage their life experiences for mentoring and volunteering, sharing their knowledge and skills to give back to the community and finding personal fulfillment in the process.

Financial Fitness: Financial planning is crucial for securing a worry-free retirement. The book outlines strategies for budget management, understanding insurance options, and preparing for potential healthcare needs.

Embracing Technology: With the digital age upon us, the book encourages older adults to engage with technology to enhance communication, learn new skills, and improve their daily lives through various digital tools and platforms.

Travel and Exploration: Travel is presented as a valuable activity for expanding horizons and experiencing new cultures, which can significantly enrich one's later years. The book offers tips for safe and enjoyable travels, whether locally or abroad.

Volunteering and Giving Back: Volunteering is shown as a means to remain active and connected while making meaningful contributions to society. The book discusses the personal and community benefits of volunteer work.

The Art of Hobbies: The significance of hobbies is emphasized as a source of joy and a means of self-expression that can also serve as a social activity to share with others.

Mindset Matters: The book underscores the importance of maintaining a positive mindset, which can transform challenges into opportunities for growth and enrichment.

Adapting the Living Space: Practical advice is provided on modifying one's living environment to ensure safety, comfort, and independence as physical needs change over time.

Navigating Health Care: Understanding and effectively using healthcare services are critical as one ages, and the book offers guidance on navigating these systems to benefit one's health.

The Legacy We Leave: Finally, the book discusses the importance of considering the legacy one wishes to leave behind, suggesting ways to impart values, knowledge, and memories that can benefit future generations.

"The Power of Positive Aging: Embracing Life After Fifty" serves as an inspirational and practical guide for anyone looking to approach their golden years with confidence and joy. By offering a diverse range of strategies and insights, it empowers readers to take control of their aging process, ensuring that these years are not only well-lived but are also rich with purpose and fulfillment.

Citation And References

This book represents the culmination of extensive research and meticulous analysis, incorporating a diverse range of sources, including numerous books, scholarly studies, and personal experiences. Additionally, I have scoured various websites to gather relevant information and data essential for the compilation of this work. I have taken every precaution to ensure the accuracy of the information presented and have diligently cited all sources to acknowledge their contributions.

Despite these efforts, the possibility of inadvertent errors remains. I deeply value the insights of my readers and appreciate any feedback that can help identify and rectify such inaccuracies. I encourage you to bring any discrepancies to my attention.

Your feedback is not only welcome but crucial, as it will aid in correcting current editions and enhancing the content of future ones. I am committed to maintaining the highest standards of accuracy and reliability in my work and thank you for your support and understanding.

Additionally, I firmly uphold the principle of freedom of speech and expression as guaranteed under Article 19(1)(a) of the Constitution of India, and I respect the diverse viewpoints and expressions of all readers.

❦❦❦

Other Books Of The Author

1. Empowering Minds: A Journey into Women's Self-Discovery and Power
2. The Dynamics of Motivation: Catalyzing Thought into Action
3. Meditation and Mental Well Being: The Path to Inner Peace and Clarity
4. The Psychology of Child Education: Nurturing Future Generations
5. Ethical Enlightenment: A Modern Guide to Living with Integrity
6. Voices of Empowerment: Stories of Women Rising Against Odds
7. Social Psychology in Everyday Life: Understanding Human Connections
8. The Essence of Motivational Speaking: Inspiring Change in Others
9. Balancing Acts: Women, Work, and the Will to Lead
10. Guiding with Grace: Raising Children with Compassion and Awareness
11. The Power of Positive Aging: Embracing Life After Fifty
12. Building Resilient Communities: Social Work in Action
13. The Ethical Educator: Principles for Teaching and Learning
14. From Insight to Impact: Social Psychology for a Better World
15. The Ethics of Empathy: A Guide to Ethical Living
16. The Science of Empowering the Self: Navigating Life's Challenges with Psychological Wisdom
17. The Mindful Conscious Leader: Meditation Techniques for Modern Management
18. Pioneering Spirit: Women's Pathways to Leadership and Empowerment
19. Feeling to Healing: The Role of Emotional Intelligence in Child Development
20. Transformative Talks and Words of Inspiration: Insights into Motivational Oratory

21. Green Ethics: A Path to Sustainable Living
22. Spiritual Integrity: Navigating Life with Moral Compassion
23. Clean Living, Clean Society: The Ethics of Cleanliness
24. Patriotic Spirits: Building a Nation on Positive Attitudes
25. Innovative Integrity & Vibrant Visions: The Ethical and Entrepreneurial Spirit of Gujarat
26. Youthful Visions, Endless Possibilities: Inspiring Ethics and Motivation in Children
27. Living Your Legacy: How to Motivate Others by Living Your Values
28. Secret of Healing Conversations: Ethical Practices in Counselling and Therapy
29. Creative Kindness: Crafting a Life of Compassion and Creativity
30. The Power of Appreciation: How Gratitude Can Transform Your Relationships
31. Bhagavad-Gita: Messages
32. Science of Art: The New Frontier of Fashion Modernism
33. Vivekananda's Virtues: A Blueprint for Modern Living
34. Empower Her: Navigating the Path to Women's Entrepreneurship
35. The Boundless Classroom: Innovations in Global Education
36. The Language of Leadership: Communicating with Authenticity and Impact
37. The Warrior's Mantra: Deciphering the Hanuman Chalisa
38. Echoes of Empathy: Transformative Stories of Social Service
39. Artful Living: Cultivating Creativity in Your Daily Routine
40. Finding Your Why: Discovering Your Passions and Charting Your Course
41. The Role of Social Media in Shaping Self-Esteem and Interpersonal Relationships among Adolescents

ৡৡৡ

Contact

Dr. Minakshi Bansal
Social Activist
Ahmedabad, Gujarat, Bharat
minakshiindiag20@yahoo.com

❦❦❦

|| LOKAHA SAMASTHAHA SUKHINO BHAVANTU ||

● 131 ●